Time and the Flying Snow

Time

and the Flying Snow

Songs of GORDON BOK

FOLK-LEGACY RECORDS, INC.   SHARON, CONNECTICUT 1977

Drawings and wood carvings by Gordon Bok
Photographs by Sandy Paton *and* Dick Levine
Music and production editing and design by Lani Herrmann

Printed at The Lakeville *Journal*, Lakeville, Connecticut
Copyright © *1977 by* Folk-Legacy Records, Inc.
Sharon, Connecticut

Library of Congress catalog card number 77-80648

Preface

About Gordon Bok

Time and the Flying Snow is just a songbook like a folksong is "just a song." Like a good folksong, this book captures a tradition and reflects a history -- the history of one person's craftsmanship in finding and creating songs and stories, translating the sounds of the squall, or the gulls, or the engine, into music, designing the instruments capable of making these songs, stories, and images come alive, and combining aesthetic judgment with technical artistry to convey what he hears in music. It is the creative synthesis of all these qualities that give Gordon Bok the unique and central role he plays in American folk music today.

Like good folksongs, Gordon's own songs -- those he has written over the past twenty years -- have evolved slowly, through many different versions and structures, with each version experiencing the wear and tear of rubbing against the individual tastes and idiosyncracies of both the creator and the listeners. One of Gordon's best songs, "Mrs. MacDonald's Lament," I first heard sixteen years ago from our mutual friend Ann Mayo Muir. The idea was there, the tune was lovely -- somewhat more wistful and less strong and urgent than the later recorded version, and the story was not spoken through the words of a particular woman. It was a good song, but it lacked the clarity of bitter complaint and the vivid dialogue which gives Mrs. MacDonald her credibility and the song its current force. Gordon tends toward the perfectionist in such matters, and his tenacity in turning such a good song into a great one is testimony to Thomas Edison's reminder that "genius is 1 per cent inspiration and 99 per cent perspiration."

The songs, cante-fables, and instrumentals in this book include the very best of the music that Gordon Bok has given us. They cut a wide swath of images, feelings, and cares. "A Tune for November" is as gentle a song of love as one could find, "Brandy Tree" as lyrically impish as one would care for. And "Herring Croon," not yet found on any of Gordon's Folk-Legacy records, is in many ways an anthem of the special respect that the fisherman has for his boat *and* his prey. "Turning toward the Morning" is here, too,

with some of Gordon's best poetry: "If I had a thing to give you, I would tell you one more time / That the world is always turning toward the morning." How could it be better said? "Bay of Fundy" (*not* "Fundy Bay") and "The Hills of Isle au Haut" -- recently a "chart-buster" in Ireland where Tommy Makem and Liam Clancy recorded it -- all these songs give us an understanding of the kinds of lives Gordon knows from the inside out and wants us to know about.

Like good folksongs, these works have emerged from the experiences of people who live on, and off of, the sea. Many of these songs, like the lives they reflect, have a somber tone. "Cape Ann" describes a voyage which nearly ended in disaster, and "Frankie on the Sheepscot" puts the title of this book in perspective: "There's nothing out there but hard times, *time and the flying snow*." Yet the strength of character, the maverick independence of the individual fisherman, and the struggle for survival with integrity -- these qualities of people have not yet been more sensitively and carefully treated than in Gordon's music.

Time and the Flying Snow also includes many of those "hard to find" songs and an occasional "hard to pronounce" song that Gordon has unearthed over the years. Among the former are Henry Lawson's poem "Freedom on the Wallaby," Charles Flower's "Broken-down Squatter," and, from his own family, "Texas Song," with its unusual and haunting melody. Among the latter are such songs as the Khasi lament "Sier Lapalang." There is continuity between these songs and those of his own creation -- the lyrical melodies, the political position of the individual, and the vivid word pictures of people doing their best to get by, relate to their friends and lovers, or find a way to keep themselves together in hard times; there is nothing frilly or trivial about these works.

And then we are graced with "Peter Kagan and the Wind," a fifteen-minute cante-fable which Gordon wrote and plays on the 12-string guitar. In this telling of Peter Kagan, marrying a seal woman, confronting the natural forces of the sea, talking to the wind as it struggles to do him in, Gordon weaves

v

many of the central ideas of his music -- the love of mystery and myth, the telling of a compelling story, the personal relationship of man with nature, and the enticing ability of the water to bring peace *or* death to those who can't shake themselves away from it. "I must go down to the sea again," wrote John Masefield in "Sea Fever," and the compelling quality of this "must" lies just beneath the surface of Peter Kagan's feeling about the sea.

Finally, this book has -- in notation and tablature -- several of the instrumentals which have given Gordon Bok his unique status as a guitarist. In my eyes, there is no more versatile and accomplished guitarist playing folk music today. Gordon has listened, closely, to guitarists from many countries, and he has integrated these varied styles into his own distinctive one. Listening to Gordon, one can hear the influences of music from South America, the Caribbean, and some aspects of classical guitar. He shares the classical bias for nylon strings and, aside from the 12-string, has not recently used a steel-stringed guitar in concert. He has no use for finger picks either, and uses a thumb pick only occasionally. Gordon's guitar style is predominantly his own creation, especially in the "handies" presented in this book.

His technical competence in stringing together fiddle tunes, jigs, and reels is impressive to the casual listener; to the musician, it's quite astounding -- accurate, seemingly effortless, inventive, quite unlike any identifiable predecessor. For all the musicians who used to be in the "How did he do that?" club, or the "Did you hear what I heard?" society, working through the instrumentals in this book should, if anything, decrease your sense of mystery about what Gordon does and increase your respect for his artistry on the guitar. And when you try these tunes on for size, remember not only that Gordon's fingers never leave his hands, but also that he has been working hard on this music for about twenty-five years.

Yet technical competence is only a part of what, for me, distinguishes Gordon's musical sensibilities on the guitar. It is more the ability to hear a sound, get inside a feeling, and translate that insight into the kind of music that makes a song more of what it really is or can be. It's a kind of self-actualization for a piece of music. For some calypso songs, Gordon has invented a way of hammering on certain frets with his *right* hand to accentuate the calypso rhythm *and* at the same time add melody notes that the left hand cannot reach. He has also patterned his playing of some of the blues -- such as Jimmy Yancey's "Death Letter Blues" -- after the way he heard it played on the piano. The piano runs, adapted to the guitar, give the blues a unique and powerful expression that enhances the statement they are making.

In this same sense, Gordon is a supreme accompanist. Listen for the harmony lines in such songs as "Mister, I Don't Mind" as they accompany the voice: the music is really a duet between guitar and voice. I wish I'd had a chance to hear him years ago when he was more frequently a "sideman" than he has recently been. My hunch is that he'd love to do more of that, adding to a song those special notes and runs that can make such a difference in how a song presents itself. Truly, Gordon knows how to listen for things like that.

As I went through *Time and the Flying Snow,* I found all these qualities in Gordon Bok's music -- the beautifully crafted words and melodies, the stories about lives that have captured his energies and his caring, and the techniques that Gordon has invented to piece them all together. If this isn't enough, there are also woodcuts that Gordon has done, and references to two instruments he developed -- the "Bokwhistle," a 6-hole whistle with interchangeable barrels to allow one to play in several keys with the same mouthpiece, and the "Bell," a pre-shrunk 12-string guitar that Gordon had a hand in developing. Like the rest of his music, these instruments were designed to provide the right texture, the right touch, for bringing out the best in songs.

In a previous life with a now defunct record company, Gordon wrote: "A song is a vessel you fill with your living." It's my privilege to be able to christen the fleet of such vessels contained in *Time and the Flying Snow.*

Ed Trickett

June 1977

Contents

If I come to you laughing, don't be fooled: it is only
the northwest wind teaching the sun to dance on scattering water,
and I, who have neither feet for dancing
     nor the strength of heart to try,
am always confounded, and the wind makes a fool of me.

If I come to you weeping, don't be sad: it is only
that I have watched too long the old moon walking
in the calling of the tides,
and I have neither the tongue to tell you
     nor the strength of heart to try,
and the years bring silence to me.

If I come to you silent, don't be turned away:
I've felt long winds around me, and strange waters turning me,
and I have no mind to understand them
     nor the strength of heart to know
I never will.

     Sometimes I feel that the angels are gone,
     for our hope and our dreaming, gone away.
     But no. We're only tired, and the angels speak so softly,
     and we lose the language of them, and we're lonely.

Mister Eneos

(The Cold South Georgia Ground)

The brig *Daisy* was the last sailing whaler out of New Bedford. This is the story, practically verbatim, that the ship's carpenter told Robert Cushman Murphy (*A Logbook for Grace* [New York: Macmillan, 1947]) about the drowning of the fourth mate, Anton Eneos.

It was told so strongly that I didn't do much to make it a song -- just rearranged some words for the sake of the meter, and added the chorus and tune.

If I remember correctly, the *Daisy* was lost with all hands a few years later off the coast of South America.

South Georgia is an island in the latitude of Cape Horn.
Guitar in A minor; recording sounds F sharp minor.
Alves = al__vesh__; Eneos = e__neeus__.

It was March twenty-ninth, Nineteen and ten, The little brig Dai-sy did sail;___

The morning was clear and the sea was down, And we raised a great pod of whale.

Clew up your royals and topsails, Haul your head-sails down,___

For you'll never see the whale no more Or the cold South Georgia ground.___

(odd verse) It struck at the boat and lifted her high, And the men fell out o-ver the stern,

And we saw the flukes come thrashing down Where Mister E-neos had been.___

2

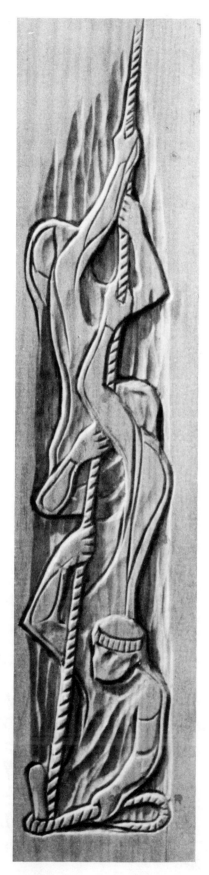

Clew up your royals and topsails,
Haul your headsails down,
For you'll never see the whale no more
Or the cold South Georgia Ground.

It was March twenty-ninth, nineteen and ten,
The little brig *Daisy* did sail;
The morning was clear and the sea was down,
And we raised a great pod of whale.

The captain had three of the boats lowered down,
And in them the mates they did go:
There was Mister Da Lomba and Mister Alves
And Mister Eneos also.

    Clew up...

Now the whales did rise a mile from the ship,
And the other two mates made their kill,
But Mister Eneos was caught in the pod
Where the whales were lying still.

Mister Eneos stood still in the bow,
And he had his lance in his hand,
But the whale he had harpooned would not break away
And would neither sound nor run.

    It struck at the boat and lifted her high,
    And the men fell out over the stern,
    And we saw the flukes come thrashing down
    Where Mister Eneos had been.

    Clew up...

The captain had the stern boat lowered away,
And we searched where the whales did sound;
Five men we gathered from out the sea,
But Mister Eneos was gone.

    Clew up...

Lou's Handy

The Boys of Blue Hill (The Boys of North Tyne)
The Reedsdale Hornpipe

Louis Killen used to warm up his whistle on these tunes, and I'd play guitar with him. One day when Louis was gone, I discovered that the guitar had learned the tunes.
A "handy" is a group of tunes played in a set.
Guitar in D and A; recording a half-tone lower.

4

5

Cape Ann

Part of this story happened to me on a little schooner quite a few years ago. When a similar thing happened to a friend of mine on a fishing vessel, I figured it was worth mixing the two stories together into a formal gripe. The names are changed and some details omitted to protect the families of the guilty.

12-string guitar in A;   recording sounds F sharp.

You can pass your days in the dory, boys,
You can go with the worst and the best,
But don't ever go with old Engleman, boys:
Each trip you go could well be your last.

Don't you remember Cape Ann, boys?
Don't you remember Cape Ann?
Oh, that crazy old drunk was a loser, boys,
He never cared if we never made in.

> *Don't you remember Cape Ann, boys,*
> *Don't you remember Cape Ann?*
> *You'll never catch me on the trawl again,*
> *For it's surely no life for a dog or a man.*

Don't you remember the Shoals, boys,
Don't you remember the Shoals?
And the Old Man asleep at the wheel, boys,
By God, it was black and cold.

Well, the mate was the man with the gall, boys,
He got the Old Man away from the wheel;
He took him below, and he locked up the hatch,
And he threw all the booze o'er the rail.

6   *(repeat first verse)*

Western Boat

("Let Me Fish off Cape St. Mary's")

Written by Otto Kelland, a warden of St. Johns Penitentiary, this song
has gone into tradition in Newfoundland. Peggy Day brought the first
three verses from Newfoundland, and Geordy Jennings brought me the rest
(Alan Mills: *Favorite Songs of Newfoundland* [Scarborough, Ontario:
Berandol Music Ltd.; copyright assigned in 1969 by BMI Canada Ltd.]).
  Guitar and recording in G.
  Hagdown: a bird.

Take me back to my western boat,
Let me fish off Cape St. Mary's,
Where the hagdowns sail and the foghorns wail,
With my friends the Browns and the Clearys
In the swells off old St. Mary's.

Let me feel my dory lift
To the broad Atlantic cumbers
Where the tide-rips swirl and the wild ducks furl
And the ocean calls the numbers...
In the swells off old St. Mary's.

Let me sail up golden bays
With my oilskins all a-streaming
From the thunder squall where I hauled my trawl
And the old *Cape Ann* a-gleaming...
In the swells off old St. Mary's.

Let me view that rugged shore,
Where the beach is all a-glisten'
With the caplin spawn, where from dusk to dawn
You bait your trawl and listen
To the undertow a-hissin'.

When I reach that last big shoal
Where the ground-swells break asunder,
Where the wild sands roll to the surge's toll,
Let me be a man and take it
When my dory fails to make it.

Take me back to that snug green cove
Where the seas roll up their thunder:
There let me rest in the earth's cool breast
Where the stars shine out their wonder
And the seas roll out their thunder.

7

Clear away in the Morning

From the days I worked on the big schooners that sail out of my home town. By the end of the summer you'd have had enough of the hours and the sound of other people's voices and you'd just want to go off by yourself for a few months. But there it would come a fine, cold day, blowing northwest, and the schooner would be stomping across the bays for home, and everything would turn around on you. You didn't want to quit; you wanted to swing her off to the westward and keep her going all winter. But no, you had to take her home, and lay her up and leave her.
Recording in B.

Take me back on the bay, boys,
  Clear away in the morning,
I don't want to go ashore, boys,
  Oh, bring her 'round.

Take me back on the bay, boys,
I don't want to spend my pay, boys.

Captain, don't you leave me,
There's no one here that needs me.

Nancy, oh my Nancy,
She never played it fancy.

Bring me wine and brandy,
I'd only ask for Nancy.

Captain, don't let the main down,
Captain, don't let the chain run.

Captain, don't you need me?
"There's nothing I can do, boy."

Nancy, oh my Nancy.
Nancy, oh my Nancy.

(repeat first verse)

Fifteen Ships on George's Bank

George's Bank is part of the great shoals of the continental shelf that have supplied our nation and many others with much of their fish for centuries. The tide runs hard across the shoals, however, and can turn the seas of a gale into an unbelievable height and steepness. In fact, many vessels were lost on the Banks by "pitch-poling," where the sea actually throws the vessel end over end. It takes quite a sea to do that to a 90-foot schooner.

I'm convinced that it was tragedies like the one in this song that helped us to change the hull form of our fishing vessels from the flatter-bottomed types, like the "mackerel-seiners," to the deeper, narrower hulls, such as we now call the "Gloucester fishermen."

Recording sounds in B flat.

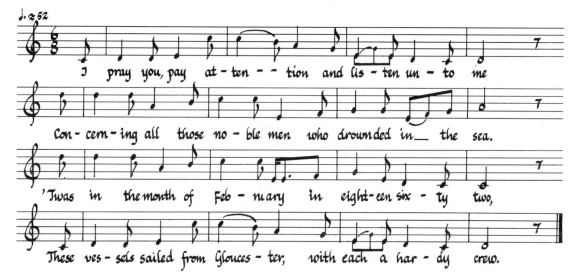

I pray you, pay attention and listen unto me
Concerning all those noble men who drownded in the sea.
'Twas in the month of February in eighteen sixty-two,
These vessels sailed from Gloucester, with each a hardy crew.

The course was east-southeast they steered, Cape Ann being out of sight;
They anchored on the Banks that night with everything all right.
But on the twenty-fourth at night, the wind come on to blow;
The seas rose up like mountain tops, which proved their overthrow.

The thoughts of home and loving ones did grieve their hearts full sore,
For well convinced were all these men they'd see their homes no more.
No tongue can ever describe the scene, the sky was full of snow,
And fifteen ships did founder there and down to bottom go.

A hundred forty-nine brave friends, who lately left the land,
Now they sleep on George's Bank, in the rough and shifting sand.
One hundred and seventy children these men have left on shore,
And seventy mournful widows their sorrows to endure.

So now you'd think with gloomy thoughts, as on life's path you roam,
Of many's the happy hours and days you've spent with them at home;
For you they left their native shore, for you the seas did roam,
For love and duty called them forth to leave their happy home.

So now adieu to George's Bank, my heart it doth despise,
For many's the gale I've seen out there, and heard those widows cry.
And now I bid you all adieu, dry up your tearful eye,
Prepare to meet your God above and dwell beyond the skies.

9

Liverpool Handy

Liverpool Hornpipe
I'ze the B'y

A friend of mine came back from fishing in the Gulf of St. Lawrence, and
he told me he was sitting in a bar in Cornerbrook when the fellow beside
him punched him in the arm and said: "How do you kill a Newfoundlander?"
    My friend says: "I dunno."
    The fellow says: "You nail his boots to the floor and play 'I'ze
the B'y'."
    Guitar in D; recording sounds a half-tone lower. The hornpipe is
ordinarily written in 2/4 or 2/2 time, but is here written as a jig to
match the second tune.
    Salts and rinds: rendered-out pork, a northeastern fisherman's
staple meal -- salts are the melted fat, rinds are what's left, and the
latter is dipped in the former.

I'ze the b'y that builds the boat,
I'ze the b'y that sails her;
I'ze the b'y that catches the fish
And takes them home to 'Liza.

    Swing your partner, Sally Thibault;
    Swing your partner, Sally Brown;
    Fogo, Twillingate, Morton's Harbor
    All around the circle.

I took 'Liza to a dance,
And faith, but she could travel,
And every step that she would take
Was up to her knees in gravel.

Susan White, she's out of sight,
Her petticoat wants a border;
Old Sam Oliver, in the dark
He kissed her in the corner.

Salts and rinds to cover your flake,
And cake and tea for supper,
Codfish in the spring of the year
Fried in maggoty butter.

(repeat first verse)

Duna

Poem by Canadian poet Marjorie Pickthall. I was pretty young when I found this poem and made the tune for it. I went off and sang it for my grandmother, rest her gentle voice, and she said something like: "That's nice, dear, but you've got the tune all wrong." A good idea gets around, I guess.

Guitar in A; recording sounds a half-tone lower. Sung very freely, with accompaniment to match. Chords in [brackets] go with the tune for the second verse.
Duna = doonah.

When I was a little lad
With folly on my lips,
Fain was I for journeying
All the seas in ships.
But I'm weary of the sea wind,
I'm weary of the foam,
And the little stars of Duna
Call me home.

When I was a young man,
Before my beard was grey,
All to seas and islands
I gave my heart away.
But now across the southern swell
Every dawn I hear
The little streams of Duna
Running clear.

12

Where Am I To Go?

Stan Hugill, in *Shanties from the Seven Seas* (London: Routledge, 1961),
says that this is a halyard chanty he heard sung with great verve and
style by a West Indian sailor named Harding.
12-string guitar in D; recording sounds in B.

Where am I to go, me Johnnies, where am I to go?
Gimme way, hey, hey, Hey, the roll and go.
Where am I to go, me Johnnies, where am I to go?
I'm a young and sai-lor lad, And where am I to go?

Where am I to go, me Johnnies,
Where am I to go?
  Gimme way, hey, hey,
  Hey, the roll and go.
Where am I to go, me Johnnies,
Where am I to go?
  I'm a young and sailor lad,
  And where am I to go?

Way out on that tops'l yard,
That's where you're bound to go....
Way out on that tops'l yard
And take that tops'l in.

Way out on that royal yard,
That's where you're bound to go....
Way out on that royal yard
That royal for to stow.

You're bound away around Cape Horn,
That's where you're bound to go....
You're bound away around Cape Horn
All in the ice and snow.

13

Bay of Fundy

This is about a long and weary, windless trip from Maine around to Halifax
on a little black schooner that seemed to move only by the slatting of her
gear. We had a coal stove in her, and the foresail used to downdraft onto
the charlienoble, turn the stack into an intake and the cabin into a
chimney. So, what with the coal gas and the wet, the offwatch was not much
more comfortable than the deadwatch.

I think the one who worked the hardest was Ed's wife, Lainie, and you
could hear her, working below or at the wheel, singing a little tune of
her own, over and over. It was a private comfort tune that probably became
as much of a comfort to the rest of us as to her.

When we got down to Cape Breton Island, I asked her if I could borrow
the tune and put words to it as a memento of the trip, and she said yes.
And I tried, all the next fall, to make that tune say what I remembered,
but after all, 'twas Lainie's tune, and private, and I had to make my own.

I tried to keep the lonely sounds, and a few notes from Sable and the
Sambro horn, but what she gave us then I have no way to give.
Guitar and recording in E minor.

14

All you Maine men, proud and young,
When you run your easting down,
Don't go down to Fundy Bay:
She'll wear your time away.
    Fundy's long and Fundy's wide,
    Fundy's fog and rain and tide;
    Never see the sun or sky,
    Just the green wave going by.

*   Cape Sable's horn blows all day long;*
*   Wonder why,*
*   Wonder why.*

Oh, you know, I'd rather ride
The Grenfell Strait or the Breton tide,
Spend my days on the Labrador,
And never see old Fundy's shore.
    All my days on the Labrador,
    And never see old Fundy's shore.

Give her staysail, give her main,
In the darkness and the rain;
I don't mind the wet and cold,
I just don't like the growing old.
    I don't mind the wet and cold,
    I just don't like the growing old.

East-by-north or east-northeast,
Give her what she steers the best;
I don't want this foggy wave
To be my far and lonely grave.
    I don't want this foggy wave
    To be my far and lonely grave.

*   Cape Sable's horn blows all day long;*
*   Wonder why,*
*   Wonder why.*

*   Cape Breton's bells ring in the swells,*
*   Ring for me,*
*   Ring for me.*

A Blues for Sergei

Sergei and I only sailed with each other once, just for a few days. We had made music off and on for a year or so because that was the only language we had in common when we met. One slow day on the boat, one of us started doodling on the guitar, making up this tune. When it was his turn to steer, the other fellow would take over the guitar and add more to it.

    It never had a name (in my mind, anyway) until Sergei died that year.

    Guitar in A; recording sounds A flat. The first part as written is a composite and is played with variations in rhythms and emphasis each time it comes around. Bass notes sound damped. The first half of each "B" part could also be played up the neck with a 5th-fret barre.

17

Mrs. MacDonald's Lament

(Windsaway)

For many reasons, among them overfishing, pollution, lack of local government control, and our general economic structure, the small-time fisherman, the jack of all coastal fishing trades, is in danger of extinction.

His credit may be good, but his creditors are caught in the squeeze, too, so after awhile he can't maintain his boat or his gear, and then he can't pay the taxes on the suddenly valuable land that his family has owned for so many generations. And so he leaves the fishing and he goes. To Florida, to the West Coast, to the cities.

But, in going, he takes with him a way of thinking, a way of living, the value of which to the world can never be measured or replaced.

12-string guitar in D; recording sounds B flat.

When the wind's a-way and the wave a-way, that cra-zy old fool will go down on the bay, Dodging the ledges and setting his gear, And come back when the wind drives him in. But he knows full well the fishing is done; His credit's all gone and the winter is come, But as sure as the tide will rise and run He'll go back on the bay a-gain.

When the wind's away and the wave away,
That crazy old fool will go down on the bay,
Dodging the ledges and setting his gear,
And come back when the wind drives him in.

> *But he knows full well the fishing is done;*
> *His credit's all gone and the winter is come,*
> *But as sure as the tide will rise and run*
> *He'll go back on the bay again.*

When the snow is down on the Western Bay,
That fool will go running the Fiddler's Ground,
Hauling his gear in the trough of the sea
As if he'd no mind of his own.

His father's gone, and his brothers are gone,
And still he goes down on the dark of the moon,
Rowing the dory and setting the twine,
And it won't even pay for his time.

When the wind's away and the wave away,
Our children go down on the morning sun;
They go rowing their little boats out on the tide,
And they'll follow their foolish old man.

> *Well, you blind old fool, your children are gone,*
> *And you never would tell them the fishing was done;*
> *Their days were numbered the day they were born,*
> *The same as their foolish old man.*

What a lot of people forget about the continental shelf is that many of
our shellfish spend at least part of their life cycles on the bottom,
out there.

So every time a few million gallons of oil are spilled and blow away
from our coast -- and we say, "Thank God for that!" -- it is sinking and
killing the lobster and crabs of the future. Actually making their growing
grounds uninhabitable.

Between the oil spills and the draggers, chewing up bottom out there
night and day, summer and winter, we can forget that particular vital (and
renewable) resource, and people like MacDonald who bring it home to us.

And won't our children be horrified to think that we allowed such a
dead-end resource like oil destroy such a perpetual one, like our fishes.

Herring Croon

Guitar in D; recording sounds in G. Originally arranged to be played on the laúdo, an instrument from the Canary Islands which resembles a little double-strung guitar tuned up to G.

Where do you go, little herring?
What do you see, tail and fin?
Blue and green, cold and dark, seaweed growing high,
Hills a hundred fathom deep where the dead men lie,
Dogfish eyes and mackerels' eyes, and they hunger after me;
Net or weir, I don't care, catch me if you can.

Where do you go, little boat,
Tar and timber, plank and sail?
I go to green bays, lift them under me;
Cold grey combing seas come to bury me;
Rocky jaws and stony claws, and they hunger after me;
Harbors cold, deep and bold: wish that I could see.

Where do you go, fisherman,
Born a sailor blood and bone?
Mackerel skies, mares' tails, reef and furl and steer,
Poor haul and hungry days, rotten line and gear,
Snow wind and winter gales, and they hunger after me;
Net or weir, I don't care, catch you if I can.

What do you see, little herring?
What do you see, tail and fin?
Blue and green, cold and dark, seaweed growing high,
Hills a hundred fathom deep where the fishermen lie,
Dogfish eyes and mackerels' eyes, oh they hunger after me;
Net or weir, I don't care, catch me if you can.

Little River

From Ruth Moore, the lady who wrote *Speak to the Winds* and *Candlemas Bay* and many other fine novels and books of poetry of the Maine coast -- and the book of "ballads" (to be read aloud rather than sung) *Cold as a Dog and the Wind Northeast*. This was a poem she wrote, another of her great and gentle bursts of light. I made the tune for it.

So many times in the fog, you stop and listen for the haunting groan of that whistle-buoy, or come down the bay all iced up from a northwest wind and that little friendly winking eye of the buoy looks so much like home you can smell the coffee, but you always know that some night you could be out there seeing it from different eyes, with that little light flicking the wavetops above you, and the looming grunt of the buoy hunting the swinging blackness around you.

For me, I hope it's as peaceful as they say it is.

12-string guitar in A minor and C; recording a half-tone lower.

22

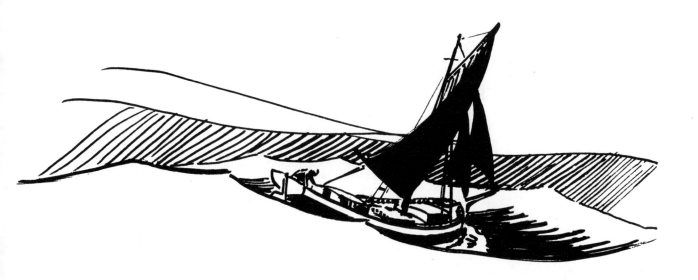

Little River lighted-whistle,
Cry no more.
Sleepy sound from the breakers calling me
Back to shore.

  Whistle it soft to the silver river,
  Whistle it loud to the drumming sea,
  Whistle it low to the moon and the morning,
  Not to me,
  Never to me.

For I'm swinging high in another country,
Swinging low.
Playing it easy, the dolphins follow me
Where I go.

  Whistle it loud to the floodtide making,
  Whistle it soft to the wheeling sun,
  Whistle it wild to my girl's heart-breaking;
  She'll remember,
  She was the one.

Spring comes warm over Little River,
Storm comes black;
I was headed home when the Indian Giver
Took me back.

  Whistle it high to the grey-beard breakers
  Where the secret over the great shoals ran;
  Whistle the world that was in my pocket
  When I had pockets,
  When I was a man.

(repeat last verse)

Gulls in the Morning

I made this tune for my good guitar-playing friend Peter Platenius. Most of it came under the influence of gull-watching from the forecastle hatch of the schooner *Steven Taber* on many bright winter mornings.

A gull is one of the best fliers of all birds, and the tune is primarily an imitation of that, rather than their speech. (You never hear a gull say anything really important, anyway.)

Guitar in D; recording a half-tone down. Order of parts: A B, A C1 C2 (without the repeat), B D C2 (with repeat), B A, end. The tremolo parts, which require from one to three well-greased fingers, flow practically without interruption.

24

26

Saben the Woodfitter

12-string guitar in A and D;   recording sounds in E flat and B flat.

Introduction

*(continue
with chords:
A, D, Bm7, E)*

When Saben the Woodfitter came for the last time
west on the western ocean,
he came alone.
And he was an old man then,
and the boat was old.

And so for the last time the black boat ran,
swung to the westward night on day,
needing neither helm nor sail-trimming,
the wind behind her.

And then one day the old man looked,
and he saw the water coming into her.
So then by the day he'd bail
and by the night he'd sleep with his hand on her keelson,
    to see when the water came.

(shift to 6/8 triplet arpeggios)

(continue with arpeggios)

And, sleeping, he heard the bell sounding the watch,
and he dreamed about the boat.
He dreamed he saw her building,
and he dreamed he saw her fishing,
and he dreamed he saw her dying in the sea.

And he rose and he went out on deck, and he said
    to the old black boat:
"Now, old boat,
I don't care for myself if ever we reach the shore or not,
but you have served me well and kindly all these many years,
and I don't want you dying in the sea.

"So I make a bargain with you:
If you will hold yourself together just a few days more,
    until we reach the land,
I promise you that I'll take you apart
    as well as I ever put you together,
plank off plank and timber from timber,
and you'll never serve a man again."

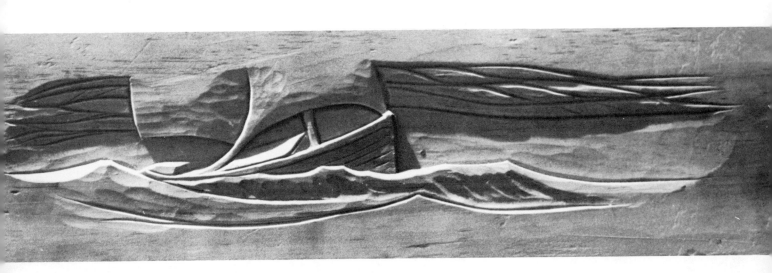

And the black boat said:
"Now, old man,
gladly have we served each other all these many years,
and gladly would I serve thee for a few days more."

And they say she took him home then,
put him on the shore.
She gave him her timbers to build his house,
her plank for his wall and her keel for his rooftree,
and she wrapped him up in her old brown sail
and laid him down,
sang him to sleep
while the winter wind came off the western ocean:

*(song accompaniment:
use triplet patterns
as in Conclusion
below)*

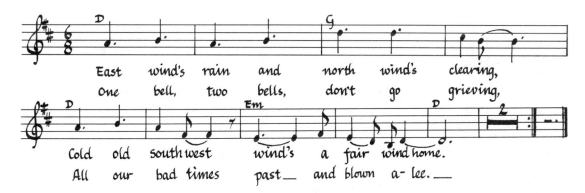

East wind's rain and north wind's clearing,
One bell, two bells, don't go grieving,
Cold old southwest wind's a fair wind home.
All our bad times past and blown a-lee.

East wind's rain and north wind's clearing,
Cold old southwest wind's a fair wind home.

One bell, two bells, don't go grieving,
All our bad times past and blown alee.

Stars thy compass, cloud thy canvas,
Rock thy keelson, wind thy course to steer.

One bell, two bells, don't go grieving,
All our bad times past and blown alee.

Conclusion

The Hills of Isle au Haut

I realized a while after I'd written this song that it was confusing some people. That wasn't what I had in mind, so I looked at it again and realized that the key word in the song is also the shortest and least significant-sounding. The word is "but."

As one fellow told me: "I know I should get out of it here, and go away. *But* I'm a fisherman, and if I'm going to starve as a fisherman, I might as well do it here where I can enjoy it."

That may be an odd way to put it, but...

Isle au Haut is a tall island in the Gulf of Maine. The place names, Plymouth, Pedro Martir (a landfall in Portugal), and Cascais were memories from a rather wet offshore trip. I enjoyed the boat, and the people were fine, and if I had grown gills I'd have been perfectly comfortable, but...

Guitar in D; recording sounds D flat.
Isle au Haut = i'll oh hoe; westward = westard; Martir = marteer;
Cascais = kass-keish.

It's away and to the westward ___ Is the place a man should go, Where the fishing's always easy; ___ They've got no ice or snow. But I'll haul down the sail where the bays come to-gether. ___ Bide a-way the days on the hills of Isle au Haut.

It's away and to the westward
Is the place a man should go,
Where the fishing's always easy,
They've got no ice or snow.

But I'll haul down the sail
Where the bays come together,
Bide away the days
On the hills of Isle au Haut.

Now, the Plymouth girls are fine,
They put their hearts in your hand;
And the Plymouth boys are able,
First-class sailors, every man.

Now, the trouble with old Martir,
You don't try her in a trawler,
For those Bay of Biscay swells,
They roll your head from off your shoulder.

The girls of Cascais,
They are strong across the shoulder,
They don't give a man advice,
They don't want to cook his supper.

Now, the winters drive you crazy,
And the fishing's hard and slow;
You're a damn fool if you stay,
But there's no better place to go.

30

Isle au Haut Lullabye

(Hay Ledge Song)

On this one, the tune came first. I was mumbling around on the guitar on deck one quiet day, and Captain Havilah Hawkins (who was to be one of the leading influences in shifting my concentration from serious sailing to serious music) told me that my greatest contribution to his enjoyment (so far) was the simplicity of my melodies. So this tune came as a guitar's most honest description of the little island we were sailing past at the time: Hay Ledge.

The words came later, a private wish of comfort for a kid who was sailing with me.

Two guitars: 6-string in C, 12-string in D capoed; recording sounds in C.

If I could give you three things,
I would give you these:
Song and laughter and a wooden home
In the shining seas.

    When you see old Isle au Haut
    Rising in the dawn,
    You will play in yellow fields
    In the morning sun.

Sleep where the wind is warm
And the moon is high.
Give sadness to the stars,
Sorrow to the sky.

Do you hear what the sails are saying
In the wind's dark song?
Give sadness to the wind,
Blown alee and gone.

Sleep now: the moon is high
And the wind blows cold,
For you are sad and young
And the sea is old.

(repeat first verse)

A Tune for November

When the wind backs a-round to the north in No-vem-ber,
Wild geese go a gang-ing out to sea; ____
There's snow on the wind. And it's e-ver been the same,
That north wind don't e-ven know my name,
That north wind don't e-ven know my name.

When the wind backs around
To the north in November,
Wild geese go a-ganging out to sea;
There's snow on the wind,
And it's ever been the same:
That north wind don't even know my name,
That north wind don't even know my name.

Long time ago
I had a pretty little girl,
She had pretty ways and silver in her tongue;
But that winter wind come prowling 'round,
That pretty girl did go,
She found a man whose house was snug and warm,
A man whose house was warm in the wind and snow.

When the wind backs around
To the north in November,
Wild geese go a-ganging out to sea;
There's snow on the wind,
And it's ever been the same:
That north wind don't even know my name,
That north wind don't even know my name.

Now the days come 'round,
I've got another kind of woman:
She's got no teasing eyes,
And her tongue is still,
And she likes the snowflakes falling,
She doesn't mind the rain,
She knows what's in her heart like she knows her name,
She knows what's in her heart like she knows her name.

I'll build her a house
Of the winds of November,
Shingled with the sun along the shore,
With the wind for her blanket,
The rain will be her door,
The pine for her pillow and her floor,
The pine for her pillow and her floor.

Song by Yupanqui

This is my "interpretation" (which means all I could figure out) of a tune made by the great Argentinian singer-guitarist-composer Atahualpa Yupanqui.
I learned it from a tape made by a friend in South America. I don't even know the name of the song, but the trying of it gave the both of us, wood and fingers, a whole new texture, a feeling, a dreaming we didn't know we had, to enjoy.
I pray the world never comes to one language, one religion, all one color, all one way of seeing the sun rise, of hearing the waves fall, because if it does I will become a slug of cement before my time (and no good to the fishes), and the guitar a club of wood. If that world comes, I don't want to live in it.
Guitar in A minor; recording sounds a half-tone lower. Order of parts: introduction, A B, A C B, A.

34

The Brandy Tree

(Otter's Song)

I learned this song from a small otter on Sherman's Point, Knox County, State of Maine, on a cold morning in 1966. Thinking it over, I wrote the refrain myself.

A thousand years (I was told) is a long time for an otter. So should it be for us.

Guitar in B-minor position; recording sounds B flat minor. The only difference between this written arrangement (in A minor) and the original is that the B-minor position, with the guitar's low E tuned down to D, permits starting the low bass run an octave down (here written in shaded notes beginning on low C), so that the run rises continuously.

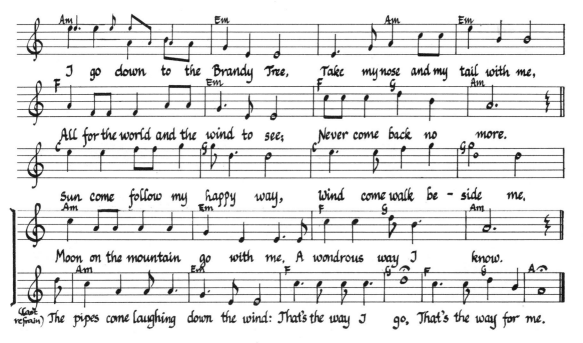

I go down to the Brandy Tree,
Take my nose and my tail with me,
All for the world and the wind to see;
Never come back no more.

Down the meadowmarsh, deep and wide,
Tumble the tangle by my side,
All for the westing wind to run
And slide in the summer rain.

Sun come follow my happy way,
Wind come walk beside me,
Moon on the mountain go with me,
A wondrous way I know.

I go down to the windy sea;
The little grey seal will play with me,
Slide on the rock and dive in the bay,
Sleep on the ledge at night.

But the seal don't try to tell me how
To fish in the windy blue;
Seal's been fishing for a thousand years,
And he knows that I have, too.

When the frog goes down to the mud to sleep
And the lamprey hides in the boulders deep,
I take my nose and my tail and go
A hundred thousand hills.

Sun come follow...

Someday down by the Brandy Tree
I'll hear the Shepherd call for me,
Call me to leave my happy ways
And the shining world I know.

Sun on the hill come go with me,
My days have all been free.
The pipes come laughing down the wind:
That's the way I go,
That's the way for me.

Sier Lapalang

38

These are the words (finally) to this song, by the kindness of the lady,
Mrs. George Allen, who first played it for me and who tried to teach me
how to sing it.

However the days fall, some are hard to everyone. I can't tell you
the peace that this song has brought to me; even in its own sorrow there
is an ancient and powerful consolation in the melody that can hold you,
no matter how hard the words try to cry to your heart. Sometimes (maybe),
it is better not to know a language.

*12-string guitar in D (low E strings tuned down to D); recording
sounds in B flat. This written arrangement, in "C open" tuning, may be
easier to play. The guitar part is a composite version.*

Ko lapalang phrang sngi jong nga
Kumba tyngshain u mangkara
Khlem sngap ki 'tien sangsot i mei
Me shem lanot ha ka pyrthei
Na snieh pyrthei shaei me phet
Sa tang marwei nga sah knunswet
Haba na nga kynrem me khlad
Dohnud sngewsih nga im suh-sat.

    *Wow la shet ka 'tieh pong deng
    Ia ka rynieng u kynremreng
    Wow la kjit u nam sarang
    Ia ka mynsiem u lapalang.*

Ko khun nga ong ynnai leit kiew
Sha ri Khasi ka ri ki briew
Shong khop ha la ri them ri thor
Bam la u khah bam la u nor
Ngin bam da u jangew jathang
Baroh shi lyiur baroh shi tlang
Pynban kynrem na nga me khlad
Marwei nga swai nga jaw ummat.

(partial translation:)
    *Mother deer tells fawn:
    Don't go to land of Khasis
    Because they'll kill you.
    Fawn didn't pay attention,
    Went anyway.
    Shot by many arrows and died.
    This is her lament.*

    *Oh, the betrayal of the bow
    Has drawn your life away,
    The stature of your beauty,
    Of the heart of the deer.*

La shat ka shanam shalyngot
Me pat hati u khadar bor
Na me ki dum ka sngi u bnai
Sha nga kumno pat men wan phai
Nampliang dusmon ia me u dung
U nam tabla u bam na krung
Pyllup me pat rangbah rangduh
Ummat aiu ngan sait khatduh.

    Kynshreng me phuh ha khmat i mei
    Mynba me ieng ha la rympei
    Na lyndet khlur mynta me sngap
    Jingud ka kmie ba shem ka pap
    Kynshreng me phuh ka khmat i mei
    Mynba me ieng ha la rympei
    Na lyndet khlur mynta me sngap
    Jingud ka kmie ba shem ka pap.

Dillan Bay

Who's to tell you where you come from? If your days were fair before you heard the ticking of other people's clocks, if you can remember what you saw and loved when only the sun or the tides governed you, *that* should be where you come from.
Guitar in D; recording sounds in F.
Dau = dow.

```
Dillan Bay, laddie-o,
dillan-dau, laddie-ay,
Dillan Bay, laddie-o,
all the boats are gone.

    Gone away, laddie-o,
    gone awa', laddie-ay,
    gone away, laddie-o,
    with their topsails high.

        Topsail high, laddie-o,
        topsail low, laddie-ay,
        topsail high, laddie-o,
        when the wind's away.

            Wind's away, laddie-o,
            wind's awa', laddie-ay,
            wind's away, laddie-o,
            down in Dillan Bay.

                Dillan Bay, laddie-o,
                dillan-dau, laddie-ay,
                Dillan Bay, laddie-o,
                all the boats are gone.
```

Hang on, John

(John Taylor)

Bob Stuart (now living somewhere in Maine) wrote this. I swiped it off him a long time ago on Long Island, so our present versions are quite different. I lean toward both versions, myself, so you may hear this one change as the years change.

Guitar in G "half-open" tuning; sounds a half-tone higher. The introduction is a composite of three phrases used in and around the accompaniment; all three are only played consecutively like this once, somewhere in the middle of the song.

Copyright 1972 by Bob Stuart.

(Some chords for this tuning:)

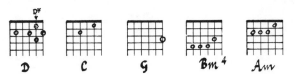

D   C   G   Bm⁴   Am

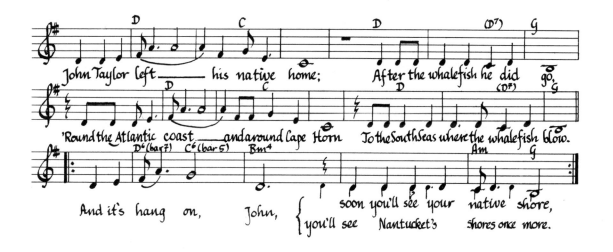

John Taylor left his native home;
After the whalefish he did go,
'Round the Atlantic coast and around Cape Horn
To the South Seas where the whalefish blow.

> *And it's hang on, John, soon you'll see your native shore,*
> *And it's hang on, John, you'll see Nantucket shores once more.*

Well, his boat was sunk, and, his luck being gone,
On a rocky island he made his home,
And he prayed and he hoped and he dreamed in vain
For a ship to carry him home again.

An old man come walking down the beach,
Harpoon in hand and a smiling face:
"I come from my home on the rolling sea
To carry you back to your native place."

So they sang and rowed, and they sang and sailed
Until they spied a newborn whale;
The old man harpooned him in the back,
And out to sea they hauled their slack.

They had not been sailing but a month or more
When "Land Ho!" was the old man's happy word,
And John saw the cliffs rising from the beach,
Heard the cry of Nantucket birds.

But they never stopped when they reached dry ground,
But they hauled their slack into John's home town,
And John got off at his own front door,
And he never saw the old man or the whale any more.

Frankie on the Sheepscot

This is about two friends of mine -- Frank Wiley and his stepfather Cleon
Stuart, from Deer Island, New Brunswick -- with whom I used to fish
occasionally. Just a picture of a particularly discouraging day towing
for shrimp on the Sheepscot River. Cleon says he wouldn't want people to
think it's always like this, and indeed it isn't, but there were many days
that particular winter when they'd end up back at the wharf by daylight,
with nothing to show for a day's work but a couple of hundred pounds of
shrimp.

The drawing is not of the boat we were fishing on, the *Elisa Glen*,
but of their sardine-carrier, the *Ida Mae*.

*12-string guitar in A; recording sounds in F. Guitar plays fairly
regular triplet arpeggios behind the song, which is sung freely and
conversationally.*

Frankie braids the purse-string, __ Cle-on sets the tow. __

Frankie goes to pick them o-ver in the well.

He's nev-er got a hat on, and the snow is all a-bout him,

And it packs a-round his head like his own skin.

"Don't I hate this foolish river!" Frankie cries; "Up and down her like a yo-yo on a string,

Go out in the morning and tear up, Mend all your after-noon,

And all this dirty riv-er__ staving by."

Purse-string: From the winch on the boat, a cable runs to a bridle on two huge iron-bound wooden "doors" that hold the mouth of the net open as it drags along the bottom. The back end of the net, the cod-end, is kept closed while towing by a couple of pucker-strings which have to be loosely braided while in use; a regular knot would never come undone when you wanted to empty the net.

Ah, but boys, you should have seen him,   Wearing the snow as you would wear your hair,

Singing: "It's a hard life____ for a boy on the Gut..."

(He's got the words wrong, but he doesn't seem to care),

And the seagulls working eas-y out be-hind him.

Cleon slides the hatch back, and he shouts down: "Boys, we're an-chored,"

And you set your cof-fee down, and you go on deck.

But the river's humping by so fast, the snow's so fly-ing thick,

You can't tell if she's moving____ or ly-ing still.

"Don't I hate this foolish river!" Frankie cries; "Up and down her like a yo-yo on a string,

Go out in the morning and tear up, Mend all your after-noon,

And all this poor old riv-er__ go-ing by...."

A boy on the Gut: Frank's "song of the week" that trip was a British tune, "It's a Hard Life for a Girl on the Cut," which he, disremembering, modified to apply to Thompson's Gut, where he and Cleon used to keep the boat.

   Anchored: The gear hung up on the bottom. What he actually said was "tanker." He had started to turn to starboard and almost ran broadside into a huge tanker coming silently up the river, a great grey wall in the snow. He cut back on the power, the net swallowed a boulder, and it was all over.

46

Frankie on the Sheepscot

Haul back: Bring the tow aboard. Whatever it was that hung us up, we
had to back and fill for awhile to get free, and when we did get the gear
up, there was nothing to do but head back in and repair it.

Tune for Bannard

I made this for a friend who was suffering from a bad case of *mal d'amour*. It's back-porch music, really, best suited for the times when all you have is a twelve-string and a thumb and finger to strum it with. (The finger may not even be necessary.) It can be played at almost any speed your engine's running at at the moment, and can certainly stand improvisation.

    12-string guitar played in D; recording sounds A flat (lower, not higher). The melody is either at the top of the strum or in the bass line. Order of parts: A (with repeat) B (repeat) C, A (repeat) to sign, hop to sign, C, A (repeat) to end, or begin again.

48

49

Threeboot Philbrick's Lament

Philbrick isn't his name, though it might as well be; this is a composite of attitudes and opinions and hummings of more than one person. I've just changed the name to indulge the guilty. It doesn't really matter who says it anyway, as long as it gets said.

He used to talk about the land as though it were a woman, and the way the different seasons made it change. He didn't care to own it, he didn't want to change it, and he couldn't understand the man that did.

The land was always there, like the wind, in his talking, and to see the young men leave it for the cities made him sad. He said a man was loaned the land for him to watch, and take care of, and he'd never (just by leaving) change his lot.

When I think of Threeboot now, I always see him laughing, but I think that underneath it he was crying for us all. So I guess it's just as well that we're rid of him at last, if we haven't got the time to try it his way.

Guitar in A; recording sounds in G. Sung very freely and conversationally, with the guitar following along.

50

But I'd just as soon be here as some-place there.

I don't need many things: lit-tle cof-fee, lit-tle rum.

And I can lie here in the cove With those lit-tle stars a-bove me,

And hear that wind running eas-y down the bay.

Go a-way, Go a-way, They tell me that it's time to go a-way.

But you're a dir-ty, hun-gry, scal-y bag of tim-bers,

And you've seen the last of your deep-wa-ter days, And I have, too.

But, by God, I'll cut us free, and we'll go a-stray to-geth-er,

And we'll try that last long voy-age, Me and you.

But there's snow on my shoes and on my head,

And there's snow on that hun-gry north-ern wind,

And you take a look a-round you: all your rambling friends are dead,

And I guess it won't be long be-fore the day comes, We go, too.

Mister, I Don't Mind

Threeboot was a happy man. He used to say, "You've got to know what's yours, and why it's good," -- and he did.

He'd seen the old fishing and the new fishing, and baled a bloodshot eye at both, for different reasons. But he'd retired, to his satisfaction, on that soggy old sloop tied up to the trees, with a chimney staggered up through her decks so he'd have most of the comforts of home (to put his feet up on, on a cold night).

And so, when someone offered him a job lumping the fish out of a sardine carrier (*lumping* as in *humping* -- the old way -- as opposed to *pumping* -- the new way), and the wind happened to be blowing northwest hard enough to crystallize a fellow's kneecaps, he took it as a personal affront. As a matter of fact, he considered the northwest wind a personal affront. I don't blame him.

Guitar and recording in A.

52

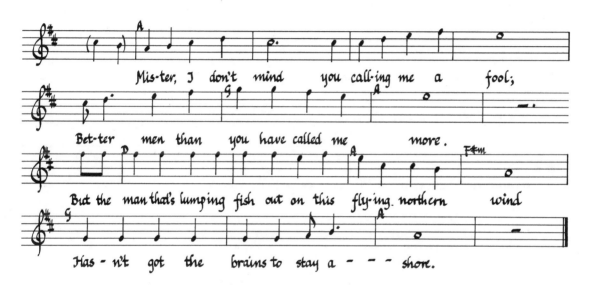

Mister, I don't mind you calling me a fool;
Better men than you have called me more.
But the man that's lumping fish out on this flying northern wind
Hasn't got the brains to stay ashore.

Lord, I think of all them boats lying down the bay,
Riding back and stretching out their chain,
And I thank my cozy toes that I ain't on them, Mister Man,
I thank the Flying Pete that they ain't mine.

Well, you know that I don't mind her beating on my door,
I don't mind her howling 'round my head,
But she drives me and she grieves me all the weary winter day,
And then she wants to share my lonely bed.

Piled the foolish snow four feet up my door,
Scaled my pretty shutters down the bay,
Took the poor old shed apart and shingled half the hill;
Now she laughs to see a grown man cry.

You know, I'm pretty sure where I'm going when I'm done,
But I'd like to send the message on ahead:
Put the coal right to her, keep her jumping up and down,
'Cause that's the way I'll want her when I come.

Dublin City

I think my uncle Gideon gave me this one. I'm told that the last two verses I sing are "uncommon." Truly they may have come from some foreign shore, and if they are the property of some fine poet (as well they may be), I hope that poet will remember the way a child will pick up odd things along the shore and put them together in ways that may be strange to others but add up to some private beauty to the child. I think that's what happened here.

12-string guitar in C; recording sounds in A flat.

As I was a-walking through Dublin City
About the hour of twelve at night,
It was there I saw a fair pretty maiden
Washing her feet by candlelight.

First she washed them and then she dried them,
And around her shoulder she pegged the towel,
And in all my life I ne'er did see
Such a fine young lass in all the world.

> *She had twenty, eighteen, sixteen, fourteen,*
> *Twelve, ten, eight, six, four, two, none;*
> *Nineteen, seventeen, fifteen, thirteen,*
> *Eleven, nine, seven, five, three, and one.*

Round, round the wheel of fortune:
Where it stops wearies me;
Fair maids, they are so deceiving,
Sad experience teaches me.

Oh, but tides do be running the whole world over;
Why, 'twas only last June month, I mind that we
Were thinking the call in the breast of the lover
So everlasting as the sea.

But here's the same little fishes that swims and spin,
And the same old moon on the cold wet sand,
And I no more to she, nor she to me,
Than the cool wind passing over my hand.

Kirsteen / Christinn

Two songs with the same name, both from Scotland, I believe. I don't remember where I heard the first one, but it was a long time ago.
  A friend told me that there is another verse to the second song, wherein it is abundantly clear that it is the girl who has died, not the man. Either way, it's very poignant.
  Two guitars ("Bell" -- high 12-string -- and 12-string); recording sounds in G.

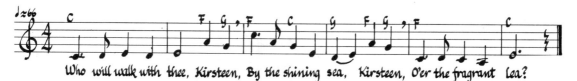

Who will walk with thee, Kirsteen, By the shining sea, Kirsteen, O'er the fragrant lea?

Who will walk with thee, Kirsteen,
By the shining sea, Kirsteen,
O'er the fragrant lea?

Who'll be by thy side, Kirsteen,
At the high spring tide, Kirsteen,
Walking with his bride?

And when thou grown frail, Kirsteen,
Winds do bring the veil, Kirsteen,
Who longs with thee to sail?

Soft be thy pathway and light be thy stepping,
Sweet be the song on thy lips, Christinn.
While lone on the hillside, thy lover is lying,
And pale is the hue of his cheek, Christinn.

Soft be thy pathway and light be thy stepping,
Sweet be the song on thy lips, Christinn,
While lone on the hillside thy lover is lying,
And pale is the hue of his cheek, Christinn.

The bird on the woodland, the trout in the river,
The deer on the hillside are fair, Christinn,
But he who was fairer lies low in the bracken;
He's emptied his heart of his cares, Christinn.

Bright blow the flowers by clear, winding cutty,
Like bonnie white clouds in the blue, Christinn,
But their glory at noontide is darkened with mourning
For joys that can never return, Christinn.

(repeat first verse)   55

Weevily Wheat

(Wheat in the Ear)

I don't know where I heard this: one of those too-far-back-to-remember
songs. I may have seen it in print and made up or borrowed the tune; if
so, I wouldn't own up to it now.
     Sometimes I sing the first line of the chorus:
     "Weevily wheat, my true love's a posy blowing..."
Guitar in D; recording a half-tone lower.

Take her by the lily-white hand,
Lead her like a pigeon,
Make her dance to Weevily Wheat
And scatter her religion.

> *Wheat in the ear, my true love's posy blowing,*
> *Wheat in the ear, I'm going back to sea,*
> *Wheat in the ear, I left you fit for sowing;*
> *When I come back, what a loaf of bread you'll be!*

I don't want your weevily wheat,
I don't want your barley;
Want some flour and a half an hour
To bake a cake for Charley.

I'm going and find a pretty little girl
Not averse to loving;
Hug her neat and kiss her sweet
And go no more a-roving.

56

Texas Song

Once again, from my mother's family. I can't remember which one of them sang it to me, but it feels like my aunt Beanto, this one. I've never heard this particular minor tune to it outside the family.
12-string guitar in A minor;   recording sounds in F sharp minor.

I'm going to leave old Texas now;
They've got no use for the long-horned cow,
They've plowed and fenced my cattle range,
And the people there are all so strange.

I'll say goodbye to the Alamo
And turn my head for Mexico,
Make my home on the wide, wide range:
The people there are not so strange.

And when my ride on earth is done,
I'll take my chance on the Promised Land;
I'll tell Saint Peter that I know
A cowman's soul ain't white as snow,
But in that far-off cattle land
He sometimes acted like a man.

Broken-down Squatter

Ray Wales, who lives in Perth, has taught me a good many grand Australian songs. He sang part of this one to me, and later sent a book to learn the rest from *(The Penguin Australian Song Book*, compiled by John S. Manifold [Penguin Books, 1964], who says this song was written by Charles Flower around the 1880's). I copied the words out and learned the tune in a vague way, but loaned or lost the book soon after, so I couldn't guarantee the tune, though the words are pretty close.
Bass guitar in A; recording sounds in F sharp.

Come, Stumpy, old man, we must shift while we can;

All your mates in the pad-dock are dead.

We must say our fare-wells to Glen E - va's sweet dells

And the hills where your master was bred.

For the banks are all bro - ken, they say,

And the mer - chants are all up a tree;

When the big - wigs are brought to the bank-rupt - cy court,

What chance for a squatter like me?

Come, Stumpy, old man, we must shift while we can;
All your mates in the paddock are dead.
We must say our farewells to Glen Eva's sweet dells
And the hills where your master was bred.

Together to roam from our drought-stricken home,
Seems hard that such things have to be,
And it's hard on a horse when he's naught for a boss
But a broken-down squatter like me.

For the banks are all broken, they say,
And the merchants are all up a tree.
When the bigwigs are brought to the bankruptcy court,
What chance for a squatter like me?

No more shall we muster the river for strays,
Or hunt on the fifteen-mile plain,
Or dash through the scrub by the light of the moon,
Or see the old homestead again.

Leave the slip-railings down, they don't matter much now,
For there's none but the crow left to see,
Perching gaunt on the pine as though longing to dine
On a broken-down squatter like me.

For the banks...

When the country was cursed with the drought at its worst,
And the cattle were dying in scores,
Though down on me luck, I kept up the pluck,
Thinking Justice might soften the laws.

But the farce had been played, and the government aid
Ain't extended to squatters, old son.
When me money was spent, they doubled the rent
And resumed the best part of the run.

For the banks...

The Cocky at Bungaree

Another good song from Ray Wales. I don't know much else about it, except a "cocky" is a farmer, in Australia, and the hero should have known what he was getting into. (A version of this is also in the *Penguin Australian Song Book*.)
12-string guitar in D; recording sounds in C.

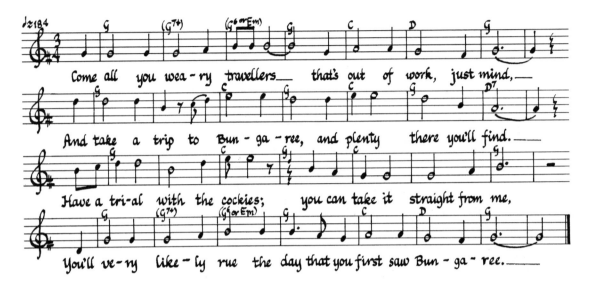

Come all you weary travellers that's out of work, just mind,
And take a trip to Bungaree, and plenty there you'll find.
Have a trial with the cockies; you can take it straight from me,
You'll very likely rue the day that you first saw Bungaree.

And how I came this weary way I soon will let you know:
Being out of employment, I didn't know where to go,
So I went to the Registry Office, boys, and it's there I did agree
To take a job at clearing for the cocky at Bungaree.

On a thirsty Monday morning, mates, it was the usual go:
He called me to me breakfast before the cock did crow;
The stars did shine most gloriously and the moon was high, you see,
And I thought before the sun would rise I would die in Bungaree.

Well, after about a week of that I reckons I'd had enough,
So I went straight up to the cocky's door and I asked him for me stuff,
And I went straight in to Bellallat, but it didn't last me long;
I went straight in to the Railway Hotel and I blew me one-pound-one.

(repeat first verse)

60

Freedom on the Wallaby

A good picture, painted by Henry Lawson, to a tune that was floating
around Australia before the turn of the century. The idea of Freedom
hooting around the Outback because she got lonely for all the hard-working
people who left England is a dear one to me. Ray Wales tells me that
"grubbing" is humping out stumps.
    12-string guitar in G; recording sounds in E flat.
    Humping bluey: to shoulder a blanket and walk the Outback;
cooey: call.

Australia's a big country, and Freedom's humping bluey,
And Freedom's on the Wallaby; oh, can't you hear her cooey?
She's just begun to boomerang, she'll knock the tyrant silly,
She's going to light another fire and boil another billy.

Our fathers toiled for bitter bread while loafers thrived beside them;
For food to eat and clothes to wear, their native land denied them,
And so they left their native land, in spite of their devotion,
And so they came, or, if they stole, were sent across the ocean.

Then Freedom couldn't stand the glare of royalty's regalia;
She left the loafers where they were and came out to Australia.
But now, across the mighty main, the chains have come to bind her;
She little thought to see again the wrongs she left behind her.

Our fathers grubbed to make a home (hard grubbing 'twas, and clearing);
They wasn't troubled much with lords when they was pioneering;
But, now that we have made this land a garden full of promise,
Old Greed must crook his dirty hand and come to take her from us.

So we must fly a rebel flag, as others did before us,
And we must sing a rebel song and join in rebel chorus.
We'll make the tyrants feel the sting of those that they would throttle;
They needn't say the fault was ours, if blood should stain the wattle.

(repeat first verse)

Paloma

"Paloma" is a Yaqui Indian dance tune from northwest Mexico. It has three basic parts, delightfully interrelated and quite powerful. The third part is usually played many times, but in the same octave, whereas I let the guitar take it into the bass, the harp's territory. It's the kind of tune that, when played for a respectably long time, becomes more and more beautiful and mesmerizing.
Guitar in D; recording sounds in C sharp.

Hatu Khara Ols'n

During the winters that I worked in Philadelphia, I became part of the band that played the traditional music of the Khalmyk (Altaic) Mongolian people that lived there, and learned some of their songs.

This was a pulling song, probably for hauling boats up a river, and some feel it originated during the time the people lived around the mouth of the lower Volga basin. It has a stronger Russian influence than their older songs show.

Because of changes in the language, the young people I learned it from couldn't translate all of it; this is only an outline, and my phonetic approximation of the words. Adding syllables in the singing, even adding them in order to lengthen the musical line as the singer wishes, is a Khalmyk style of singing.

Learned from Sara (Stepkin) Goripow and Nadja (Stepkin) Budschalow.
Recording sounds in A.

Hatu khara ols'n
Hak'run badje tatulau.

Hak'run badje tatuschen
Har'mshdele edje minje saanugdna.

Idje linje irgede kudluschen
Injegem ondzin nandan, saanugdna.

I pull the hard black rope and I sing.

Mother
Father
My people
My country
} *In the far land I do not forget you.*
While this river runs, I do not forget you.

63

Ed McDermott's Handy

Cherish the Ladies
Garryowen
Haste to the Wedding

64

Edward McDermott, the grand Irish fiddler, who so happily taught us all so much, taught "Cherish the Ladies" to Lani Herrmann (the precise and patient soul who put all this musical confusion into the order you see now). I "learned" the tune by accompanying Lani, but (I found later) with a glorious disregard for particulars.

If Ed could see now, though, how much of his magic keeps trying to find its way into every note I play, I think he'd forgive me some of my notical transgressions.

"Garryowen" and "Haste to the Wedding" are also tunes that Ed McDermott played, though I learned them from Charlie Richards of Camden, Maine, who used to be a fiddler in the "Old New Englanders."

Guitar played, and recording sounds, in D.

66

La Brigantine

The Canadian French often preferred the brigantine rig to the schooner, for cargo and fishing. Here they speak of it as the ship of death: a funeral chant.

I learned it when I was quite young, but forgot the melody, so I asked Shirley Ruffalo (Brown) to read it for me, and took the shape of this tune from her inflection.

Recording in F sharp minor. Guitar sounds a funereal drone, more percussive than harmonic.

La Brigantine qui va tourner,
Roule et s'incline
Pour m'entraîner.

Ah, Vierge Marie,
Pour moi priez-Dieu;
Adieu, Patrie,
Québec, adieu.

*The Brigantine that goes,
rolling and pitching,
takes me with it.*

*Oh, Virgin Mary,
pray to God for me.
Goodbye, my country;
Goodbye, Quebec.*

Snow Gull

("The Seagull of the Land-under-Waves")

This one changes with the singing; I can't remember where I heard it.
It was printed in *Songs of the Hebrides*, Volume I (London: Boosey, 1909)
by Marjorie Kennedy-Fraser. She described it as "an old Skye air from
Francis Tolmie, with words from Kenneth Macleod."

Both Ireland and Scotland have legends of a land to the westward of
them which is the dwelling place of the souls of the dead. In this case
the land is underwater, and the gull is its guardian.

"Bell" guitar in its G, Bokwhistle in F; recording sounds B flat.

Snow-white seagull high,
    Hoo-ay dee,
Tell to me
Where, ah, where thou rest them,
    Hi, heeray o-ho,
Where our fair young lads are resting.
    Horen eiry-oh,
    Hoo-ay dee,
    Ho eiry-oh,
    Ho, hey, horen eiry,
    Hi, heeray o-ho,
Grief within my heart is nesting,
    Horen eiry-oh.

Heart to heart they lie,
Side by side,
Sea-foam the sign
From their cold lips coming;
Sea-wrack their shroud
And their harp the cold sea moaning.
    Horen eiry-oh,
    Hoo-ay dee,
    Ho eiry-oh,
    Ho, hey, horen eiry,
    Hi, heeray o-ho,
Grief within my heart is nesting.
    Horen eiry-oh.

Snow-white seagull high,
    Hoo-ay dee,
Tell to me
Where, ah, where thou rest them,
    Hi, heeray o-ho,
Where our fair young lads are resting.
    Horen eiry-oh,
    Hoo-ay dee,
    Ho eiry-oh,
    Ho, hey, horen eiry,
Sea-wrack their shroud
And their harps the cold sea moaning.
    Horen eiry-oh,
    Hoo-ay dee,
    Ho eiry-oh,
    Ho, hey, horen eiry,
    Hi, heeray o-ho,
Grief within my heart is nesting.
    Horen eiry-oh.

Turning toward the Morning

One of the things which provoked this song was a letter from a friend who had had a very difficult year and was looking for the courage to keep on plowing into it. Those times, you lift your eyes up unto the hills, as they say, but the hills of northern New England in November can be about as much comfort as a cold crowbar.

You have to look ahead a bit, then, and realize that all the hills and trees and flowers will still be there come Spring, usually more permanent than your troubles. And, if your courage occasionally fails, that's okay, too; nobody expects you to be as strong (or as old) as the land.

12-string guitar in A with low E strings tuned down to D; recording sounds in G.

When the deer has bedded down, and the bear has gone to ground,
And the northern goose has wandered off to warmer bay and sound,
It's so eas-y in the cold to feel the darkness of the year;
And the heart is grow-ing lone-ly for the morning.

Oh, my Joan-ie, don't you know that the stars are swinging slow
And the seas are roll-ing eas-y as they did so long a - - go?
If I had a thing to give you, I would tell you one more time
That the world is al-ways turning toward the morning.

When the deer has bedded down
And the bear has gone to ground,
And the northern goose has wandered off
To warmer bay and sound,
It's so easy in the cold to feel
The darkness of the year,
And the heart is growing lonely
For the morning.

Oh, my Joanie, don't you know
That the stars are swinging slow,
And the seas are rolling easy
As they did so long ago?
If I had a thing to give you,
I would tell you one more time
That the world is always turning
Toward the morning.

Now October's growing thin
And November's coming home,
You'll be thinking of the season
And the sad things that you've seen;
And you hear that old wind walking,
Hear him singing high and thin:
You could swear he's out there singing
Of your sorrows.

When the darkness falls around you
And the North Wind comes to blow,
And you hear him call your name out
As he walks the brittle snow:
That old wind don't mean you trouble,
He don't care or even know,
He's just walking down the darkness
Toward the morning.

It's a pity we don't know
What the little flowers know.
They can't face the cold November,
They can't take the wind and snow:
They put their glories all behind them,
Bow their heads and let it go,
But you know they'll be there shining
In the morning.

Now, my Joanie, don't you know
That the days are rolling slow,
And the winter's walking easy
As he did so long ago?
And if that wind should come and ask you,
"Why's my Joanie weeping so?"
Won't you tell him that you're weeping
For the morning?

O Wyrak'ocha!

Slow Dance from Macchu Picchu, Peru

We now think the proper name for this dance tune is "Ô Wyrak'ocha!" (O white man," literally "O sea-foam"). I heard it on a tape of an unidentified group from the Macchu Picchu area, recorded by a friend. It was played on the local cane flutes and assorted other instruments, and this version is my reconstruction of it from memory, using the instruments we had.

Only those who know and love traditional South American music will know how much of it is lost in translation, but I hope the joy and dignity of the tune will come through to hold you as it has held me.

Two C Bokwhistles played in F; high guitar in C, low guitar in G; recording sounds in F. This arrangement is a composite skeleton taken from the recording, on which the full tune is played once through by solo and duet whistles and guitars, then once again (with the first section played only once) as a guitar duet. In fact, it can be played, with permutations and combinations, until exhaustion sets in. The guitar chord accompaniment is rolled throughout; the rhythm is steady and stately.

Bheir Me O

My aunt Beanto (Boericke) Cohen gave me this lovely thing. She sang me
many songs from the Scottish Hebrides when I was growing up -- to help me
keep my feet off the ground, I think.
12-string guitar in D; recording sounds in B flat.
Bheir = vair; cruit mo chruidh = chroosh mo chree.

Bheir me O, ho-ro van-oh, Bheir me O, ho-ro van-ee,
Bheir me O, o hoo-ro ho, Sad am I with-out thee.

Bheir me O, horo van-oh,
Bheir me O, horo van-ee,
Bheir me O, O hooro ho,
Sad am I without thee.

Thou'rt the music of my heart,
Harp of joy, *O cruit mo chruidh,*
Moon of guidance by night,
Strength and light thou'rt to me.

In the morning, when I go
To the white and shining sea,
In the calling of the seal
Thy soft calling to me.

When I'm lonely, dear white heart,
Black the night and wild the sea;
By love's light my foot finds
The old pathway to thee.

74

Peter Kagan and the Wind

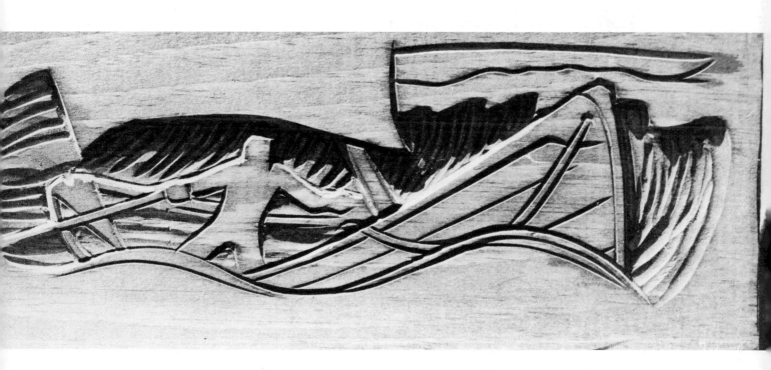

12-string guitar in A and E minor; recording sounds a half-tone lower. The main themes are written here as if for 6-string guitar, but certain of the sounds (such as the gong-buoy) are unique to the 12-string, where the strings, in pairs, are tuned an octave apart and played either individually or together.

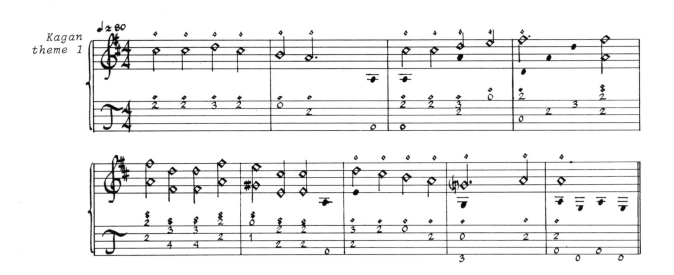

Kagan theme 1

Kagan theme 2

Peter Kagan and the Wind

Introduction
Kagan theme 1

Peter Kagan was a lonely man, in the summer of his years.
But then one day he got tired of being lonely,
so he went away off to the eastward,
and, when he came again, he had a wife with him.

She was strange, you know, but she was kind,
and people liked her.

And she was good for Kagan, she kept him company,
and, winter come to summer, they were happy.

Kagan had a dory then, had a lugsail on her mast.
He'd go offshore for three, four days, setting for the fish.

But oh, his wife was sad then;
she never liked to see him go.
She'd go down and call to him:

Ka - gan, Ka - gan, Ka - gan,   Bring the do - ry home.
The wind and sea do follow thee, And all the ledges call - ing thee.

Kagan, Kagan, Kagan:
Bring the dory home.
The wind and sea do follow thee,
And all the ledges calling thee.

Kagan theme 2

He said that he could hear her singing twenty miles to sea,
and, when he heard her, he'd come home,
if he had fish or none.

She was a seal, you know.
Everyone knew that; even Kagan, he knew that,
but nobody would say it to him.

Then one day in that year's autumn, Kagan says:
I got to go now, go offshore and get some fish.

But she says: No -- don't go away.
She starts crying:
Please don't go -- The wind is coming, and the snow.

Kagan, Kagan, Kagan:
Don't go out to sea.
The stormy wind and snow do come,
And oh, but I do fear for thee.

But Kagan's not afraid of snow; it's early in the year.
He puts his oars in, and he goes to sea.

77

Sailing 1

Sailing 2
and
Rowing 1

Gong-buoy

Gong-buoy
and
Kagan
theme

78

Peter Kagan and the Wind

Kagan sails out on the Middle Ground.   *Sailing 1*
The wind is west all day, and going down;
the fish are coming to him.

Kagan reads the writing on the water and the sky.
He sees the haze, up very high, above the clouds.
He says: That's all right for autumn,
only a change of wind. I'm not afraid of wind.

But Kagan reads it wrong this time.   *Sailing 2*
The wind goes away, and then comes back southeast.   *+ Rowing*
The fog comes 'round him.   *(repeat chords*
                                                         ad lib.)

Kagan says: I better go now.
Find that gong-buoy off the Sunken Ledges.
Then I'll know the best way home.

He puts the sail up, and he bears away to the northward
for the gong.

But oh, the wind is watching. The wind backs 'round   *(Rowing,*
to the eastward, and breezes on.   *louder)*
They sail a long time, and the sail is pulling very hard.

Finally the wind's so strong the sail tears out.
Kagan takes it in, and the dory goes drifting.   *(fade)*

But then he hears the gong-buoy;   *Gong-buoy*
it isn't very far away.

        Kagan, Kagan, Kagan: *Gong-buoy*
        Bring the dory home.   *+ Kagan theme*
        The wind and sea do follow thee
        And all the ledges calling thee.

But the dory goes drifting;
Bye and bye the buoy goes away.   *(Gong-buoy*
                                                         fades)

Kagan says, Okay.
He puts the oars in, starts to row back up for the gong.

But oh, the wind is watching.
The wind backs 'round northeast, and makes the sea confused.   *(Kagan*
                                                               + Rowing)

The wind says: Listen, I got something to tell you.
Kagan, rowing: I don't want to hear it.

But the wind humps up -- makes the seas short,   *(harder)*
makes it hard for him to row.
Finally the seas are so steep Kagan knows he isn't getting
anywhere. He takes the oars in,
and the dory goes drifting, now.   *(fade)*

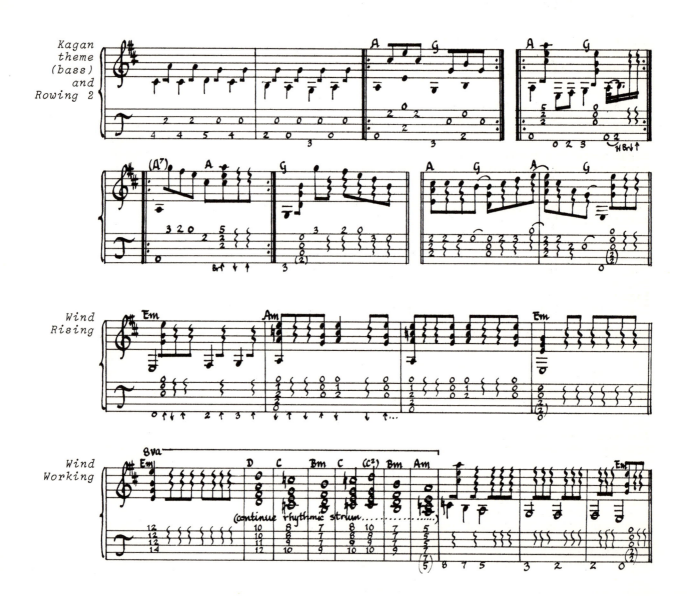

Kagan
theme
(bass)
and
Rowing 2

Wind
Rising

Wind
Working

80

Peter Kagan and the Wind

*Kagan theme (bass)
+ Rowing 2
(variations:
mix and repeat
sections)*

Kagan says: Okay, now I got something to show you.
He takes a slip of wood to make a needle,
waxes up the handline for a thread --
sews the sail up smaller, sews a reef in it.

Wind says: What you doing?
Kagan says: You keep watching.

Kagan puts the sail up now,
bears away to the northward for the gong.

But oh, the wind is watching now.
The wind backs north-northeast.
Kagan can't hold his course now.

Kagan says: Okay, then.
He brings the boat about; now he's steering east.

The wind says: You're heading out to sea.
Kagan says: I'm not afraid of water.
I'll come about, bye and bye, when I can fetch that gong.

The wind says: I'll veer on you; I'll go east again.   *Wind Rising*
Kagan says: You go ahead.   Then I can hold my course again.   *(repeat
ad lib.)*

The wind says: I'll back.
Kagan says: You back too far, and you'll have to clear.
You know that. I can keep ahead of you.

Wind says: You may be smarter, but I'm stronger.
You watch.
Wind gets bigger, blows harder.   *Wind Working*

Finally there's too much wind.
Sail says: I can't do it.
Kagan says: I know that. Thank you.

He takes the sail in, and the dory goes -- drifting.   *(fade)*

Wind Rising (triplets).

Modulation: Gong-buoy to Kagan theme

(continue triplets)

(continue triplet pattern......)

(continue triplet pattern........................)

Peter Kagan and the Wind

Kagan takes the sail off the yard.
He pulls it round him: Now, you keep me warm.
The wind says: He can't keep you warm.

Wind snatches off north-by-east: I'll freeze you.
Kagan says: I'm not afraid of cold.
But Kagan is afraid. He doesn't know what to do.

But oh, the wind is working now;
the wind brings ice and snow,
the wind blows long, and long, and black.

Kagan says: I'm dying. Sail, keep me warm.
Sail says: I can't do it, Peter.

Kagan dying, and the wind blows.

> *Kagan, Kagan, Kagan:*
> *Turn thee now to me;*
> *Turn thy back unto the wind*
> *And all the weary, windy sea.*
>
> *Kagan, Kagan, Kagan:*
> *Lay thee down to sleep,*
> *For I do come to comfort thee,*
> *All and thy dear body keep.*

So Kagan lies down in the bottom of the boat,
and tries not to be afraid of the dying.

And he dreamed of her then, of his wife.
He dreamed she was coming to him.
He heard a great calling down the wind,
and he lifted his head, and he saw her coming.
Over the rail of the dory she came, and laughing,
to his arms.

And all in the night and the storm they did lay,
and the wind and the sea went away.

And in the morning they found him,
asleep, with the sail wrapped 'round him.
And there was a seal lying with him, there,
curled over him like a blanket --
and the snow was upon the seal.

*(continue
Wind Rising
in triplet
arpeggios)*

*(add Wind Working
to build up
a storm)*

(fade)

*Modulation:
Gong-buoy
to Kagan theme*

*(Sailing 2,
a little faster
then fade)*

(Kagan theme 2)

*(Conclusion:
second half of
Kagan theme 1)*

Transforming a tune from a record-ing into visible symbols involves choosing what to write down and in what form. The transcriptions in this book are meant for people who want to learn these songs and instrumental pieces; we hope they are clear enough to be read by themselves and detailed enough to permit following the recordings. But some explanation of the conventions chosen may also be helpful.

The music for the songs follows the words as written out (generally, the first verse and refrain); it may need to be adapted to subsequent verses so that the words have their proper value and meter. Some melodic varia-tions are added in small notes, or whole variant sections are written out. Refrain texts, printed in *italics*, are written out only once unless the text varies or the refrain does not follow every verse.

Some instrumental introductions and whole guitar parts have also been written out, to present ideas for ac-companiment patterns and material that can be used to build accompaniments and interludes. These may amount to an entire guitar solo, but more often the guitar becomes a second voice for the song, another line (or three) to weave into the texture of the tune.

Pitches and keys are a little tricky. The guitars on the recordings like to be tuned to their own pitches, often lower than standard tuning (EADGBE), so both the chord positions played and the actual pitch heard on the recordings are given here: play-ing along may involve retuning, trans-posing, or using a capo. The guitar parts are written as if they were to be played in standard pitch, with unusual tunings indicated as used. The vocal parts with guitar have also been brought to equivalent standard pitches. Some arrangements have been moved to a different key to facilitate reading or playing, with due notice given. A few use the "treble tenor" clef, 𝄞 , where the notes and inter-vals are the same as in the treble clef but an octave down.

Music notation has been modified somewhat to minimize clutter and to make the structure of the arrangement (melody, harmony, rhythm) easier to see and follow.

Key signatures reflect the notes in the tune, not necessarily the nomi-nal or formal key (for which, see the chord symbols). Thus, for example, "A Blues for Sergei" is nominally in A, three sharps, but is written with only one sharp because of the "blue" seventh (G, not G#) and "weak" third (which wobbles between C and C#).

Major chords are labeled: "A", and minor chords: "Am." Chords in parentheses are optional. Chords on guitar parts are intended to guide ac-companying instruments as well as to aid in deciphering the parts or working out new ones. But chords have been left out in a few cases where they seemed superfluous.

Time signatures and barlines cus-tomarily indicate strong beats and convenient rhythmic (and visual) di-vision. A time signature in paren-theses means some odd-sized measures (extra pulses) are present, and these are set off by dotted barlines. Dot-ted barlines are also used as a visual aid in parts with no regular meter (e.g., Kagan's gong-buoy).

The indication ♫ = ♩♪ means the piece goes "with a bounce," as in hornpipes and (differently) blues; the rhythm is not really as square and even as written. The metronome indi-cations are supposed to be helpful, not absolute.

Dynamics are indicated only when they seem essential.

On the guitar parts:

1. The tablature is basically that used in contemporary American pub-lications ("Seeger tab"), here with

each space on the staff representing a string and the numbers indicating the frets (counting up from the open string as zero) to be fingered. Because the tablature follows under the standard notation fairly precisely, the rhythmic notation ("stems and flags") has not been duplicated on it.

   2. Accompaniment bass notes are written without stems if they fall on the beat; but offbeat eighth (etc.) notes may be written with flags pointing backwards toward the beat they follow: ♩♪

   3. Simple accompaniment patterns may be started and then dropped or abbreviated, with due notice.

   4. A "strum" sign on the staff (𝄎) implies a (quick) strum on the last previous written-out finger or chord position: a kind of repeat sign. A note written on a strum sign (see "Tune for Bannard") is a melody note which should be heard over the strum.

   5. Other symbols used (most of them standard):

⟋ₛₗ. = left-hand slide up

⟍ₛₗ. = left-hand slide down

 = , arpeggio or roll "up" (low to high strings and notes; written on the music staff)

T or ↓ = right-hand strum "down" (also low to high strings; written under the staff)

↑ = right-hand strum "up" (high to low strings; written under the staff)

H = "hammer on" (note sounded with a finger of the left hand)

P = "pull off" (note sounded with a finger of the left hand)

ρ = harmonic note; (♩) indicates the actual note sounded; $\frac{o}{5}$ in tablature, the position to be touched

ρ = "octavado" harmonic produced by fretting a note normally with the left hand and, with the right, both touching the harmonic point (12 frets above the left-hand note) and sounding the note; in tablature $\frac{o}{3}$ indicates the left-hand position

ρ = double octavado, the same as above but for two simultaneous notes; $\frac{o}{3}\frac{o}{2}$ in tablature

♬ ≡ = tremolo (There are several kinds, as well as several techniques for producing them on the guitar; the pragmatic approach is probably best: listen carefully to the recordings and do whatever works and sounds best.)

(3) (ρ) = notes fretted but not necessarily sounded

   6. Grace notes are usually played on the beat, rather than before.

A note on instruments

   The "Bell" is a small bell-shaped 12-string guitar developed by Sam Tibbetts, Gordon Bok, and Nick Apollonio of Camden, Maine.

   The 6-string, 12-string, and bass guitars are Bok designs, also built by Nick Apollonio.

   The "Bokwhistle" is a soft-voiced form of traditional 6-hole whistle designed and built by Gordon Bok.

Acknowledgments

   Special thanks are offered to Marlene and Dick Levine for help with proofreading and reference-hunting, and again to Dick for his generosity and expertise in darkroom matters.

Lani Herrmann
June 1977

Index of titles and first lines

(Numbers in parentheses refer to Folk-Legacy recordings.)